Dinosaur Shapes

by David West

Crabtree Publishing Company
www.crabtreebooks.com

Published in 2013 by CRABTREE PUBLISHING COMPANY

Author: David West
Editor: Crystal Sikkens
Editorial director: Kathy Middleton
Prepress technician: Margaret Salter
Cover design: Margaret Salter
Image credits: David West
Cover credits: Shutterstock (background); David West

Library and Archives Canada Cataloguing in Publication

West, David, 1956-
    Dinosaur shapes / David West.

(I learn with dinosaurs)
Issued also in electronic formats.
ISBN 978-0-7787-7456-3 (bound).--ISBN 978-0-7787-7461-7 (pbk.)

    1. Shapes--Juvenile literature. 2. Dinosaurs--Juvenile literature.
I. Title. II. Series: West, David, 1956- I learn with dinosaurs.

QA445.5.W43 2013   j516'.15   C2012-908502-2

Library of Congress Cataloging-in-Publication Data

CIP available at Library of Congress

Crabtree Publishing Company

www.crabtreebooks.com   1-800-387-7650

Printed in Canada/012013/MA20121217

Published in Canada
Crabtree Publishing
616 Welland Ave.
St. Catharines, Ontario
L2M 5V6

Published in the United States
Crabtree Publishing
PMB 59051
350 Fifth Avenue, 59th Floor
New York, New York 10118

Published in the United Kingdom
Crabtree Publishing
Maritime House
Basin Road North, Hove
BN41 1WR

Published in Australia
Crabtree Publishing
3 Charles Street
Coburg North
VIC, 3058

◯ Circle

Billy goes riding with the Dracorexes and Hypsilophodons.

How many circles can you see on his bike?

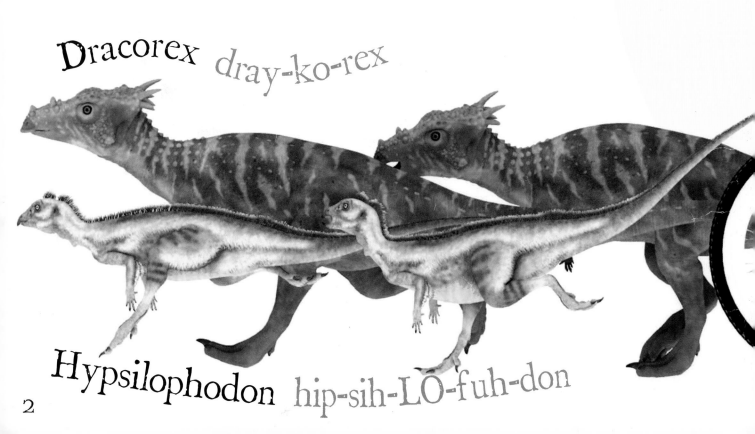

Dracorex dray-ko-rex

Hypsilophodon hip-sih-LO-fuh-don

Triceratops

try-SAIR-uh-tops

△Triangle

Stop! A Triceratops is crossing the road.

Can you see the triangle road sign?

☐ Square

Come back! The Heterodontosaurus has taken Mia's chess piece.

Heterodontosaurus
het-er-uh-DON-tuh-SAWR-us

Can you find the blue square?

☐Rectangle

Kate and Joe chase after the Archaeoceratops.

How many rectangles can you see?

Archaeoceratops ar-kee-o-SAIR-uh-tops

Oval

The Anchisaurus is getting too close to Billy's oval sunglasses.

Anchisaurus   ANG-kee-SAWR-us

Can you find six ovals?

●Sphere

Mia plays soccer with three Troodons.

Which object in the
picture is a sphere?

Troodon TRO-uh-don

Pyramid

Mia and Aadi visit Egypt with the Camarasaurus.

How many pyramids
can you see?

Camarasaurus   kuh-MARE-uh-SAWR-us

Cube

The Europasaurus helps
Billy and Emma make
a pile
of cubes.

There are eleven cubes.
Can you find
them all?

Europasaurus

yoo-ro-pa-SAWR-us

Prism

Mia and Joe have set up their tents for camping. The Citipatis want to share.

Citipati   chit-ee-puh-tee

Can you see
the prism
shapes here?

Cone

The Stegocerases follow Billy as he rides between the traffic cones.

How many cones can you find in this picture?

Stegoceras steg-OSS-er-us

Cylinder

An Olorotitan is walking among the cylinders at the building site.

There are five cylinders.
Two of them are yellow.
Can you spot them all?

Olorotitan   oh-LOW-ruh-tye-tan

Can you remember the names of all these shapes?